The Adventures of Monty, The Dog Who Wears Glasses

Colin West

Monty, the dog who wears glasses; Monty Bites Back; Monty -
up to his neck in trouble first published by A & C Black (Publishers) Limited
1989, 1990, 1991

First published in one volume as The Adventures of Monty,
the dog who wears glasses in Young Lions 1993

Young Lions is an imprint of the Children's Division,
part of HarperCollins Publishers Ltd,
77/85 Fulham Palace Road, Hammersmith,
London W6 8JB

Copyright © Colin West 1989, 1990, 1991

The author asserts the moral right to be
identified as the author of this work.

Printed and bound in Great Britain by
HarperCollins Book Manufacturing, Glasgow

Contents

Monty, The Dog Who Wears Glasses

The Reason Why

This is Monty. He looks rather
unusual.

I bet you're wondering why I'm wearing glasses.

MONTY

Well, one day, before Monty took to
wearing glasses, he was taking
young Simon Sprod for a walk.
He was waiting for Simon outside
the sweet shop, when he *almost*
had a nasty accident.

A man on a bicycle swerved to avoid
Monty, and only *just* managed to
keep his balance.

Simon rushed out. The man looked over his shoulder as he rode off, and shouted:

What that dog needs is a pair of glasses!

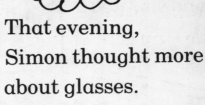

That evening,
Simon thought more
about glasses.

Not that Monty was
short-sighted or anything, but
a pair of glasses might help to
remind him of his near-accident.
They might make him more careful
in future.

So Simon found an old pair of
sunglasses and took out both lenses.
Then he put them on Monty's nose.

Monty didn't like the glasses much.
They pinched his nose and felt
uncomfortable. So Simon loosened
the tiny screws in the hinges and
eased the ear-pieces wider apart.

That did it. They fitted perfectly.
Everyone agreed that Monty looked
even more handsome now.

And even more
intelligent, too!

But the new glasses didn't seem to cure his habit of accidents.

12

Monty's Barbecue

Mr and Mrs Sprod had visitors.
This was bad news for Monty, as
there were fewer chairs to go round.

Still, it wasn't *all* bad news.

The Sprods were good hosts. There was a lot of laughter and there was talk of a barbecue in the garden if the rain held off.

Monty loved barbecues more than anyone because they meant his favourite food –

15

He was soon on the patio.

'Look at Monty!' Mrs Jackson cried.
'Oh, he always does that in the nice
weather,' said Mrs Sprod.
'Shall we join him?' someone else
suggested.

Soon Mr Sprod had put on a frilly apron and taken charge of cooking the sausages.

Mrs Nutford was Monty's favourite visitor. She was a vegetarian, although she was too polite to refuse food that was given her.

But Monty didn't do so well with
other people.

Suddenly it started to rain
and everyone ran back indoors.

At last Monty came in, dripping wet.

Monty at School

It was Monday morning and the Sprod children, Simon and Josie, were off to school.

That morning, Monty sneaked out
of the back door and followed Simon
and Josie down the street. No one
took much notice of him, and he was
able to follow them all the way.

Simon and Josie hurried into school.

Monty lost sight of them.

Which way did they go?

23

Monty took the first corridor.

Inside a large room, he found
some comfy chairs.

And soon
he was
fast asleep.

Monty was having a lovely dream
about a huge chocolate cake,
when he was woken by a very loud
electric bell.

RINNNGGG!

Soon the room was invaded by . . .

. . . lots of funny-looking grown-ups.

Then they all began trying to guess
where Monty had come from.
Some of them made a fuss of him,
while others were less friendly.

Then a little face peered round the door. It was Mary Worth from Class 1, and she'd come to the staffroom to hand in some lost property.

Of course she saw Monty sitting there. Soon the news was spreading around the playground.

Simon and Josie realized it could
only be Monty. They went rather
nervously to claim him.

Monty was glad to see some
familiar faces.

Mrs Prendlethorpe, the
headmistress, was glad to get the
matter sorted out.

She made it plain that she didn't
want Monty in school again.
But just this once, he was allowed to
sit at the back of the classroom . . .

. . . and later to have some school dinner . . .

. . . and then to join in a game of rounders.

Mrs Prendlethorpe needn't have worried about Monty visiting again. Although he liked the comfy chair, he didn't care for the rest of the day's activities.

Monty at the Library

Josie was off to buy her mum a
newspaper. She'd got some letters to
post first, and Monty had the job of
carrying them to the post box.

Everyone they passed was most
impressed, and Monty felt quite
proud.

Josie popped the letters into the box
and then bought the newspaper.
Monty carried it all the way home.

Everyone was just as impressed as
before, and Mrs Sprod gave Monty
a chocolate biscuit for being so
helpful.

In the afternoon, Monty heard
Mrs Sprod reminding Simon to
return a library book which was due
back that day.
Simon would
have to pay a
fine if the book
was late.

Maybe this is
my chance to
earn another
biscuit!

So when no one was looking, Monty took the book between his teeth and sneaked out of the house.

He made his way to the library.
People stopped to stare at him as he
went by.

A dog with glasses
carrying a book—
how novel!

At the corner of Tower Road,
there was a big puddle
on the pavement.
As Monty was edging his way round it...

... someone in a passing car hooted at him.

And as Monty yelped in surprise . . .

the book fell into the muddy puddle.

Monty retrieved it and gave it a
good shake to dry it off.
But the pages were still a bit soggy.

Monty reached the library and
climbed the steps with the book
safe and sound. He presented it
eagerly to the lady behind the desk.

But the lady didn't look too pleased.

She took the book between finger
and thumb, and looked at the
damage.

Then she picked up a pen and wrote
a note for Monty to take away.

Monty found Mrs Sprod in the
living room on her hands and knees.
He dropped the note in front of her.
'What's that?' asked Simon,
who was also on all fours.

Mrs Sprod looked at the note.
'It's from the library,' she said.
'It's about that book we've been
looking for all afternoon.'

Then she read aloud.

Monty didn't get another chocolate
biscuit that day.

Monty's Christmas

It was Christmas Eve.

Soon Father Christmas would be coming down the chimney.

'Who is Father Christmas, anyway?' Monty wondered.

When Simon and Josie were
in bed . . .

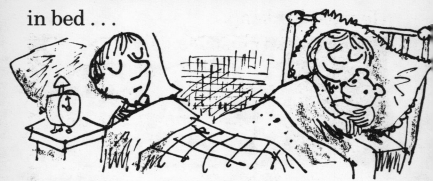

. . . and Mr and Mrs Sprod were
watching TV . . .

. . . Monty was
in his
basket in
the kitchen.

But he wasn't sleeping.
He was thinking.

Monty decided he'd help out.
He padded into the living room.

Good! Everyone's gone to bed!

Monty sat down by the fireplace
under the coloured lights of the
Christmas tree. He waited for
Father Christmas to arrive.

He waited . . .

and waited . . .

and waited.

Suddenly, Monty was disturbed by
someone walking round the room.

'That's funny,' he thought, as he
opened one eye. 'The man's got
a sack all right, but he hasn't got
a big white beard.'

Monty leapt up and nipped the
burglar on the ankle.

Then Mrs Sprod came down to
find out what was the matter.
She came into the living room and
switched on the light.

Monty got a big surprise.

The man with the sack was
Mr Sprod.

'I was just putting the presents
round the Christmas tree and that
daft dog attacked me!' he moaned,
still rubbing his ankle.

Monty was amazed. Mr Sprod, it seemed, was really Father Christmas.

Monty could have kicked himself –
he'd missed seeing Mr Sprod come
down the chimney.

How on earth
he finds time to
deliver everyone's
presents and work
at the office, I'll
never know!

Monty at the Supermarket

Mrs Sprod was at the entrance to the supermarket.

'I'll only be ten minutes,' Mrs Sprod
told Monty, as she took a trolley
from the line and went inside.

Monty hated waiting.
The supermarket looked so inviting.
He could see bright lights and
people having trolley races.

After a few minutes, the man
in charge of trolleys came out and
added some stray ones to the line.

The trolley man had his own names for most of the regulars.

The trolley man went away again and Monty carried on waiting.

Monty eyed the line of trolleys.

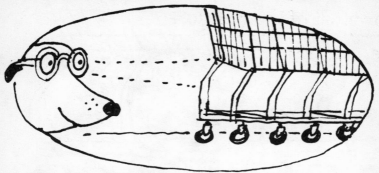

'Maybe I could get up into one of
those,' he thought.
So he slipped his collar and had a go.

As soon as he'd settled down, a lady
in a fur coat came along and hauled
Monty's trolley out of the line.

She didn't notice Monty. She wheeled the trolley inside.

This is what I call luxury!

Soon Monty was in the warm, and there was the sound of soothing supermarket music.

Monty was sitting in the bottom
part of the trolley – and the lady
was loading tins into the top part.
'She's bought nothing but cat food,'
thought Monty.

They were soon at the check-out counter. The girl at the till began taking tins of Katty-Kit out of the trolley. She didn't notice Monty . . .

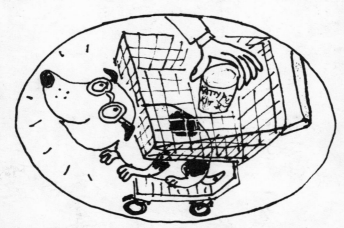

. . .until she took out the last tin.

'No dogs allowed in the store!'
she told the fur-coated lady.
'Really!' shrieked the lady.
'Do I look the sort who'd have a
scruffy old mongrel like *that*!'

At least I don't have a moth-eaten coat!

Just when things were getting
nasty, a man with a moustache
came over and settled the argument.
He seemed to be the manager,
and he took Monty into his office.
Monty prepared himself for a
ticking-off.

But the manager turned out to be
friendly. He was in the middle of
morning tea, and he gave Monty his
slice of fruit cake.

Monty was finishing
the last mouthful
of cake, when the
trolley man came in.

The trolley man said that the dog
with the specs had been reported lost
from the Dogs' Waiting Area.
The manager himself took Monty
back to Mrs Sprod. She looked
relieved but embarrassed.

Mrs Sprod fastened Monty's collar.
'Really! Why can't you be patient,
like these other dogs?' she said.
'I've had more fun than *them*,'
thought Monty.

And I can highly recommend the fruit cake!

Monty Bites Back

Monty Gets the Chop

Simon and Josie Sprod were
worried that Monty was just as
clumsy as ever.

They'd made Monty a pair of
glasses to remind him to look where
he was going, but he still seemed
accident-prone.

'From now on, every time you cause an accident, we're going to put it in the book,' said Simon.

'And if you get three mishaps in one day, you're in for the chop!' said Josie.

Monty had to make sure he was
extra careful from now on.
He walked round the house
very cautiously.

But then at lunchtime, Monty was careless. When getting a sausage that someone had left on their plate . . .

. . . he pulled off the tablecloth . . .

. . . and most of the things on it.

It all went down in the book.

Later, on his way to the garden,
Monty knocked over the pot plant
in the hall.

That went down in the book, too.

Monty was really worried now.
One more mishap, and he'd be in for
the chop.

He hardly dared move, in case he
knocked something over, or spilled
something, or put his foot in
something.

In the end, Monty just sat in his basket while Mrs Sprod got on with the cooking.

You're very quiet this evening, Monty. Are you all right?

Before Monty could open his mouth, Mrs Sprod took a dish from the oven. It smelled delicious.

'Oh dear, I've cooked too much
meat,' murmured Mrs Sprod.
'Here, Monty, as you're being so good,
you can have the chop.'

'How very confusing!' thought
Monty as he licked his lips.

Monty's Picnic

It was a beautiful sunny day and
the Sprod family were going on a
picnic. Monty was dozing in his
basket.

'Now, have I got everything?' asked Mrs Sprod as she examined the hamper.

Vacuum flask, plastic cups, serviettes, egg sandwiches, mince pies...

Suddenly Monty sat up.

Did someone say **mince pies?**

Mr Sprod took the hamper to the car.
Simon and Josie helped to tie it on.

Mrs Sprod locked up the house and
then they were off.

The Sprods' house

They went for miles and miles and miles and miles and miles.

To the Seaside

N
W   E
S

82

And after two hours . . .

Mrs Sprod noticed they were getting low on petrol.

Josie spotted a garage.

Mrs Sprod drew up and got out
to work the pump. Mr Sprod and
the children went to investigate
the shop.

When Mrs Sprod went to pay
at the till, Monty clambered through
a back window . . .

. . . and on to the roof of the car.

He sniffed the hamper.

There was no stopping him.
He nudged open the lid, hopped in
and got to work on the pies.

By the time Monty was on his fifth
mince pie, he heard voices from
below.

Before he could do anything,
the car started up.

VRROOOOM!

Monty held on to the sides of the
hamper as the car sped along.
He only just managed to duck in
time for a bridge.

They went round lots of bends...

...and over lots of bumps.

'Is Monty enjoying the ride?' asked Mrs Sprod. For the first time, Simon and Josie looked down at the empty space between them.

'WHAT!' exclaimed Mr Sprod.
The car screeched to a halt.

It was such a sudden jolt that
Monty and the picnic food were
hurled from the hamper.

Mr Sprod got out. He was quite angry.

That dog must have been sitting inside the hamper.

Monty looked ill.

The vacuum flask is broken.

The food is ruined.

But Monty's safe – that's the main thing.

'Let's go to the sea-side anyway,' said Mrs Sprod. 'We'll find a nice snack bar.'

So that's what they did.

But guess who couldn't eat another thing all day!

Monty and the Cat Next Door

Gertrude, the cat next door, was really getting on Monty's nerves. She got all the attention these days.

She's had more tickles under the chin than I've had hot dinners.

One afternoon, Gertrude was preening herself by her front gate. Monty had noticed her through a gap in the fence.

Monty squeezed through the gap
and crept up behind Gertrude.

Then he let out his most ferocious
bark.

RRRUUFFF!

The terrified cat almost jumped out
of her skin.

Monty yapped some more, and the cat took off. Gertrude leapt through the bars of the front gate.

Monty set off after her.

But he wasn't quite as slim as
Gertrude. His head got through the
bars, but not the rest of him.

Try as he might, he couldn't budge.

Before long, a small crowd gathered round Monty.

Then a woman with a shopping basket had a bright idea.

Carefully, she removed Monty's glasses. Then she rubbed some margarine behind his ears.

Monty simply pulled his head free!

Everyone cheered and made a
tremendous fuss of him.

And Monty was the talk of the
neighbourhood for weeks.

Monty and the School Fête

It was the day of Josie and Simon's school fête. All the proceeds were going to the School Orchestra Fund. Lots of stalls had been set up on the school playing field.

There were unusual games with
prizes for the lucky winners . . .

There was a white elephant stall.

There was a home-made cake stall.

There was a second-hand book stall.

And there was Simon and Josie's craft stall.

They'd made little animals out of
scraps of material . . .

ONLY 50p. EACH

. . . and paper-weights out of pebbles.

Hand painted

They'd knitted egg cosies . . .

IDEAL GIFT!

. . . and they'd made interesting jewellery out of bits and pieces.

BROOCHES

Necklaces

'Dear Monty' Earrings

The trouble was, not many people seemed interested in buying anything from them.

It's three o'clock, and we've only sold one egg cosy.

And that was to Mr and Mrs Sprod!

At half past three, the headmistress, Mrs Prendlethorpe, came along to see how things were going. Mrs P had met Monty before.

'Hello, Miss,' said Simon and Josie.
'Hello, children!' Mrs Prendlethorpe
said, trying to ignore Monty.

Then she looked down. 'Just keep
your dog out of mischief,' she said to
Simon in a quiet voice.

Monty heard Mrs Prendlethorpe
say she was off to help out at the
cake stall. He decided to follow her.

If I can get
into her good books,
I might get some
free samples!

But then, as Monty was wondering
how he could impress the
headmistress, a sudden gust of wind
almost knocked him off his feet.

Whoosh!

The gust swept off Mrs P's hat, and carried it away.

Help! My new hat!

Monty seized his chance and chased
after the hat.

He raced through the crowds.

He had to run fast, but was just about able to keep up with it.

Then, with one almighty leap, Monty pounced and caught the hat in his teeth!

A loud cheer went up. When Monty looked round, he saw that everyone had been watching him.

HOORAY!

Monty made his way back to the cake stall, and returned the hat to Mrs Prendlethorpe. She seemed to be the only person who wasn't smiling.

Simon came over and apologised.
He took Monty back to the craft stall.

Josie sat Monty on a chair, so she could keep an eye on him. But she soon noticed people coming over to meet the dog who'd saved the headmistress's hat.

And everyone who came wanted to
buy a souvenir.

By the end of the afternoon, Simon and Josie had sold everything in sight! They were able to hand over £37·97 for the School Orchestra Fund. The good news cheered up Mrs Prendlethorpe no end.

Monty's Mistake

One Friday afternoon, Mrs Sprod was reading a magazine . . .

. . . Josie was reading a book . . .

. . . and Simon was reading a comic.

Mrs Sprod was reading about diets.
Suddenly she said:

I'm very worried about your father. According to this article, he's nearly two stones overweight.

Just then Monty passed by the door.

Mrs Sprod went on:

From now on, I won't give him second helpings.

Monty thought Mrs Sprod was talking about *him!*

And he'll have to make do without his chocolate biscuits.

Gulp!

'I think you
should cut
down on his
sausages, too!'
said Josie.
'Good idea,'
said Mrs Sprod.

'And don't give
him so much
fruit cake!'
said Simon.
'That's a good
idea, too,'
said Mrs Sprod.

Monty gulped some more.
He didn't like the sound of this.

Monty plodded off and wondered what to do.

But then he'd miss his comfy basket.

At last, Monty decided he'd have to show everyone that although he was podgy, he was still super-fit.

Monty prepared himself for his first
move. That evening, when Mr Sprod
came home from work, Monty
bounded down the garden path
and almost knocked him over.

Then Monty started yapping loudly.

Then he started dancing round
Mr Sprod, and even managed a few
somersaults.

He's never done
that before.

Then he raced round Simon
seven times.

Monty was getting tired, but he
decided to do his most spectacular
feat of all . . .

He jumped up on to the bird bath
and tried to do a hand stand . . .

Unfortunately, Monty lost his
balance and toppled into the pond.

Simon pulled out a bedraggled Monty.

Everyone crowded round Monty,
who was shivering.

So Josie took Monty inside.

Josie tucked Monty up, snug and
warm. Then she fetched the biscuits.

Monty was amazed. His plan had
worked after all!

Monty -
up to his neck in trouble

Monty's Toothache

One morning Monty, the dog who
wears glasses, had a bad dream.
He dreamt that all his teeth fell out
just as he was about to bite into
a juicy steak.

It was terrible!
Monty didn't have a tooth left in
his head.

Then, in his dream, a mad professor
(who looked a bit like his owner,
Mr Sprod) fitted him with a set of
false teeth.

The story even made the evening paper, the *Nightmare News*.

MONTY- THE DOG WHO WEARS DENTURES

Local dog Monty has been fitted with a revolutionary device— a set of false teeth. The new gnashers are the brainchild of Prof. Sprodski, who replaced Monty's original when they fell out.
owners, Josie

Monty shows off his ne

Monty woke up in a cold sweat. He was relieved to find it was all a dream, but he had the most dreadful toothache all the same.

Maybe my teeth really are about to fall out!

'How awful!' thought Monty.
'Maybe I'll have to wear false teeth
in real life.'
There would be no more steaks
or toffees or bones or biscuits.

Monty was so worried he couldn't
touch his breakfast.

He couldn't even be tempted by his favourite chocolate biscuits.

The pain went on all day and just wouldn't go away.

In the end, Mr Sprod decided Monty
would have to visit the vet.

The waiting room made Monty feel
even worse.

He sat between a sick parrot and
a lizard covered in spots.

At last it was Monty's turn.
Mr Sprod explained what was wrong.

The vet prodded and probed Monty
for a full five minutes.
Monty didn't enjoy it.

Then the vet decided to take a look inside Monty's mouth.

Accidentally Monty nipped her fingers.

Monty's ears pricked up.

Suddenly Monty was full of beans.
He started wagging his tail and
licked the vet's hand to show that
he was sorry.

As they said goodbye, Monty forgot
about his toothache.
'I wonder what's for dinner?' he
thought. 'I haven't had a bite all day.'

Monty at the Movies

It was a wet afternoon and Mrs Sprod
and the children were out shopping
with Monty.

'Look!' cried Simon, 'The cinema is showing *The Four-Eyed Monster From Mars!*'

'Hey, Mum, it's about to begin – can we go in?' pleaded Josie.

'Oh, all right,' said Mrs Sprod.

I suppose it will get us out of the rain. But keep quiet about Monty – I don't think they like dogs!

Mrs Sprod bought the tickets.
Luckily the cashier didn't notice
Monty . . .

Neither did the usherette . . .

They settled in the front row.
Monty snuggled down under a seat.
Before long the lights dimmed and
everyone held their breath, waiting
for the film.

At least
it's dry in
here!

First of all there were a few adverts.
One went like this:

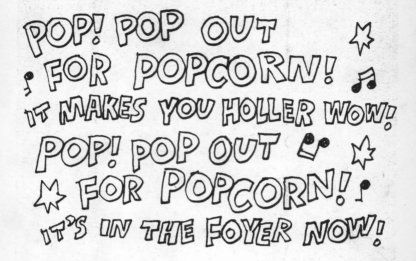

The words really got into Monty's
brain.

Soon he was in a trance.

Dreamily Monty wandered off into the darkness.

He headed up the aisle. Monty could still hear those words in his head . . .

No one noticed Monty, as by now the film had begun.

But Monty was hypnotised.

He could see a
bright light in the
distance, and was
drawn towards it.

When Monty
reached the
back row,
he leapt up
on an empty
seat, and
then onto
the wall
behind it.

He walked along, getting closer
and closer to the light.
Suddenly Monty was dazzled.
At the same moment, the whole
audience gasped.
Silhouetted on the huge screen
were Monty's monstrous features.

Monty came out of his trance.
He blinked a lot, toppled from his
perch, and landed on someone's lap.

'It's the Four-Eyed Monster from
Mars!' cried her boyfriend, running
away.

Everyone turned round.
Monty hardly knew where he was.
He jumped from one seat to another,
scattering people as he went.

When Monty reached the front row,
Simon and Josie caught hold of him.

'Quick, we'd better leave before we get thrown out,' whispered Mrs Sprod.

In the daylight Josie sighed: 'Huh, Monty really spoiled the film.'

'Oh well,' said Mrs Sprod, 'at least it's stopped raining now. Let's head for home.'

As they passed a sweet shop, Simon suggested: 'Can we pop in for something, Mum?'

'Pop!' thought Monty . . .

POP POP POP!

Monty's Party Adventure

Simon and Josie were off to their
friend Fiona's birthday party.

Monty knew all about parties.
He knew there was always lots of
food – sausage rolls, crisps,
sandwiches, and best of all,
chocolate cake covered in icing.

When Josie and Simon had left, Monty tried to settle down, but he couldn't help thinking of all that delicious party food.

Fiona lives just round the corner.

I'm sure she wouldn't mind me paying a surprise visit.

If I put on my 'sorrowful look,' she's bound to give me some birthday cake!

Monty's mouth was watering.
He sneaked out the back door.

He climbed on to the dustbin and
clambered over the fence.

Then he crossed next-door's garden,
and burrowed under a hedge,

and then went past a funny statue,

and then hopped on to a wheelbarrow
and leapt over a wall.

Then Monty went across the next garden, and squeezed through a gap.

Monty got a bit entangled in a washing line in the next garden. He had to shake off a tea towel which fell on his head.

But soon he was off again, heading
for a hole in the hedge.

Monty squeezed through and
wandered on to a neatly cut lawn.

He trampled over a flower bed and
made his way to the big house
at the top of the garden.

Monty guessed where Fiona and her guests would be and went up to a window. He could just make out some figures sitting at a table.

Monty tried to get a better view.

But what Monty didn't know was
that he was at the wrong house.

He'd gone wrong when the tea towel
fell on him. He was now at
Mrs Perkins-Smythe's house, where
she was giving a tea party.

Just then, Mrs Perkins-Smythe
caught sight of Monty's nose pressed
against the window pane.

Before Monty could run off, the vicar ran outside and caught hold of his collar.

'Look who I've caught!' the vicar said triumphantly on his return.

At last Monty realised he was at the wrong house.

But soon everyone was crowding round him and feeding him cakes.

Monty had a nice snooze until
finally the guests thought it was
time to leave.

It's been lovely!

'Please allow me to return Monty,'
volunteered the vicar.
'Yes, by all means,' replied
Mrs Perkins-Smythe.

The vicar left with Monty under his arm. As he was at the front gate, he bumped into Josie and Simon.

They had just come from Fiona's house nearby, and were on their way home.

The vicar explained how Monty
had brightened up the tea party.
'Thanks for looking after him,' said
Josie.
'You're most welcome,' replied the
vicar. 'Now goodbye, children, and
goodbye to you too, Monty.'

What a kind
man — it must
be the 'dog collar'!

Monty at the Park

One hot summer's day, Simon, Josie and Monty went to the park to feed the ducks.

When they reached the lake, Simon
tied the end of Monty's lead to a tree.

Simon and Josie went to the water's edge and started throwing crusts. Soon they were surrounded by lots of ducks.

Meanwhile Monty was getting bored. He'd sniffed the tree, and walked round it four times. Now there didn't seem much else to do.

Monty sat in the shade and looked
longingly at the ice cream stand in
the distance.
He started licking his lips at the
thought of an ice cream.
But how could he get one?

People kept passing by, licking ices.
Monty was getting more and more
thirsty . . .

On the horizon he saw a man carrying
a soft ice cream that looked as if it
might melt at any moment.

Monty began to drool.

The ice cream grew bigger . . .

. . . and bigger . . .

. . . AND BIGGER!

Monty jumped up to snatch a lick.

Just at that moment Monty's lead
jerked up and the man tripped head
over heels.
The ice cream flew out of its cone . . .

. . . and straight down Monty's throat.

Mmmm . . . it was strawberry –
Monty's favourite!

As the man brushed himself down,
Monty noticed he looked rather angry.

Just then, Josie and Simon came back from feeding the ducks.
'You should keep that dog under control!' the man shouted, before storming off.

Monty in Trouble

One Monday morning after Simon and Josie had gone to school, Mrs Sprod noticed Josie had left her recorder behind.

Monty looked sadly at the recorder
and started thinking . . .

When Mrs Sprod wasn't looking,
Monty took Josie's recorder in his
mouth and crept out of the house.

Monty had visited School before, so
he knew the way, and he raced
along the streets.

As Monty reached School, he saw the Headmistress, Mrs Prendlethorpe, at the entrance. She was looking out for latecomers.

Monty found an open door, but as soon as he entered, he heard someone shout:

A woman waving a ladle started chasing Monty.

Monty jumped up on a table, and
dashed along a work top, then tried
to leap over a big pot.

But he didn't make it.

He fell in up to his neck.

Josie's recorder sank to the bottom,
as Monty splashed about frantically.

At last Monty scrambled out and
darted through the nearest door.

Just then the Headmistress came to
see what the commotion was about.
'A funny dog got into the custard,'
explained a dinner lady.
Mrs Prendlethorpe's face dropped.

He wasn't wearing
glasses by any
chance, was he?

Why, yes!

Mrs Prendlethorpe realised it could
only be Monty.

The women followed a trail of custard along the corridor until they found Monty cowering outside Josie's classroom.

Mrs P. asked Josie to explain things.

Suddenly the Headmistress didn't look so cross.

Mrs Prendlethorpe went away
looking much happier.
A little later, at dinner-time, she
announced that everyone would have
fresh fruit today instead of pudding.

A lot of children found they preferred
fruit . . .

Mrs Prendlethorpe was so pleased,
she even fished out Josie's recorder
and cleaned it up so Josie could join
in with Music Practice after all.

Then Mrs Prendlethorpe phoned
Mrs Sprod to tell her that Monty was
safe and sound, and gave him his very
own lunch – a nice healthy apple.

The Three Investigators Mysteries

Meet the Three Investigators – brilliant Jupiter Jones, athletic Pete Crenshaw and studious Bob Andrews. Their motto, "We investigate anything" has led them into some bizarre and dangerous situations. Join the three boys in their sensational mysteries, available only in Armada.

Enid Blyton
Five Find-Outers
Mystery Stories
in Armada

Anastasia Krupnik is a totally engaging and precocious heroine, whose considerable insight and self-confidence generally keep her on top of her world, in spite of an occasional slip. By Lois Lowry.

Anastasia Krupnik
Anastasia comes to terms with having a baby brother.

Anastasia Again!
Anastasia and her family move to the suburbs and make friends with their elderly neighbour.

Anastasia, Ask Your Analyst!
Anastasia realises that the problem is herself, so she undertakes a course with Freud.

Anastasia at Your Service
Bored and broke, Anastasia decides to work as paid companion to a rich old lady and finds the job not quite what she had expected.

Anastasia has the Answers
Well, most of them! But one thing she knows she'll never master is climbing the ropes in the gym...

Anastasia on her Own
When her mother goes to California for ten days, Anastasia is left in charge of running the house.

Anastasia's Chosen Career
Anastasia feels she needs self-confidence, so enrols on a modelling course. But somehow she's not cut out to be a model.
All at £3.50

Have you read all the adventures in the "Mystery" series by Enid Blyton? Here are some of them:

The Rubadub Mystery
Who is the enemy agent at the top-secret submarine harbour? Roger, Diana, Snubby and Barney are determined to find out – and find themselves involved in a most exciting mystery.

The Rat-A-Tat Mystery
When the big knocker on the ancient door of Rat-A-Tat House bangs by itself in the middle of the night, it heralds a series of very peculiar happenings – and provides another action-packed adventures for Roger, Diana, Snubby and Barney.

The Ragamuffin Mystery
"This is going to be the most exciting holiday we've ever had," said Roger – and little does he know how true his words will prove when he and his three friends go to Merlin's Cove and discover the bideout of a gang of thieves.

The Rubadub Mystery	£2.75
The Rat-A-Tat Mystery	£2.99
The Ragamuffin Mystery	£2.75

Have you read all the adventures in the "Mystery" series by Enid Blyton? Here are some of them:

The Rockingdown Mystery
Roger, Diana, Snubby and Barney hear strange noises in the cellar while staying at Rockingdown Hall. Barney goes to investigate and makes a startling discovery...

The Rilloby Fair Mystery
Valuable papers have disappeared – the Green Hands Gang has struck again! Which of Barney's workmates at the circus is responsible? The four friends turn detectives – and have to tackle a dangerous criminal.

The Ring o' Bells Mystery
Eerie things happen at deserted Ring o' Bells Hall – bells start to ring, strange noises are heard in a secret passage, and there are some very unfriendly strangers about. Something very mysterious is going on, and the friends mean to find out what.

The Rockingdown Mystery	**£2.99**
The Rilloby Fair Mystery	**£2.99**
The Ring o' Bells Mystery	**£2.99**

The Chalet School Series
Elinor M. Brent-Dyer

Elinor M. Brent-Dyer has written many books about life at the famous alpine school. Follow the thrilling adventures of Joey, Mary-Lou and all the other well-loved characters in these delightful stories, available only in Armada.

Chalet School Three-in-One (containing *The Chalet School in Exile*, *The Chalet School at War*, and *The Highland Twins at the Chalet School*) £4.99

Have you seen the Hardy Boys lately?

You can continue to enjoy the Hardy Boys in a new action-packed series written especially for older readers. Each book has more high-tech adventure, intrigue, mystery and danger than ever before.

Join Frank and Joe in these fabulous adventures, available only in Armada.

The Jinny Books
Patricia Leitch

When Jinny Manders rescues Shantih, a chestnut Arab, from a cruel circus, her dreams of owning a horse of her own seem to come true. But Shantih is wild, and almost imposs-ible to manage. Jinny perseveres, and she and Shantih have many very exciting adventures.

For Love of a Horse	£2.99
A Devil to Ride	£2.99
The Summer Riders	£2.99
Night of the Red Horse	£2.99
Gallop to the Hills	£2.99
Horse in a Million	£2.99
The Magic Pony	£2.99
Ride Like the Wind	£2.99
Chestnut Gold	£2.99
Jump for the Moon	£2.99
Horse of Fire	£2.99
Running Wild	£2.99
Jinny 3-in-1	£4.99

(contains *For Love of a Horse,
A Devil to Ride* and *The Summer Riders*)

Have you seen Nancy Drew lately?

Nancy Drew has become a girl of the 90s! There is hardly a girl from seven to seventeen who doesn't know her name.

Now you can continue to enjoy Nancy Drew in a new series, written for older readers – THE NANCY DREW FILES. Each book has more romance, fashion, mystery and adventure.

In THE NANCY DREW FILES, Nancy pursues one thrilling adventure after another. With her boundless energy and intelligence, Nancy finds herself enrolling at a crime-ridden high school, attending rock concerts and locating the missing star, skiing in Vermont with friends Bess and George and faithful boyfriend Ned, and temping at a teenage magazine based in wildly exciting New York.

 1 Secrets can Kill   £2.99
 2 Deadly Intent   £2.99
 3 Murder on Ice   £2.99
 4 Smile and Say Murder   £2.99
 5 Hit-and-Run Holiday   £2.99
 6 White Water Terror   £2.99
 7 Deadly Doubles   £2.99
 8 Two Points to Murder   £2.99
 9 False Moves   £2.99
10 Buried Secrets   £2.99

The Chronicles of Narnia
C. S. Lewis

Each of the seven titles is a complete story in itself, but all take place in the magical land of Narnia. Guided by the noble Lion Aslan, the children learn that evil and treachery can only be overcome by courage, loyalty and great sacrifice.

In reading order:

The Magician's Nephew	**£3.50**
The Lion, The Witch and the Wardrobe	**£3.50**
The Horse and His Boy	**£3.50**
Prince Caspian	**£3.50**
The Voyage of the _Dawn Treader_	**£3.50**
The Silver Chair	**£3.50**
The Last Battle	**£3.50**
Narnia Gift Pack	**£25.00**

(all seven titles in a slipcase)

The Chronicles of Narnia are also available in larger format editions, price £3.50 each (the slipcase is £25.00, and contains all seven titles) and in hardback, price £6.95 each. The boxed hardback set is £50.00.

Scrambled Legs
Jahnna N. Malcolm

ROCKY: hot tempered
MARY BUBNIK: worst dancer ever
GWEN: shortsighted and sharp-tongued
McGEE: softball fanatic
ZAN: head permanently in the clouds

Five friends at Deerfield's Academy of Dancing. What do they have in common?
Nothing – except they all hate ballet!

Order Form

To order direct from the publishers, just make a list of the titles you want and fill in the form below:

Name ....

Address ....

....

....

....

Send to: Dept 6, HarperCollins Publishers Ltd, Westerhill Road, Bishopbriggs, Glasgow G64 2QT.

Please enclose a cheque or postal order to the value of the cover price, plus:

UK & BFPO: Add £1.00 for the first book, and 25p per copy for each additional book ordered.

Overseas and Eire: Add £2.95 service charge. Books will be sent by surface mail but quotes for airmail despatch will be given on request.

A 24-hour telephone ordering service is available to Visa and Access card holders: 041-772 2281